# CRADDOCK'S
# *Cranky Coloring Book*

## Artwork and Designs by John Ward

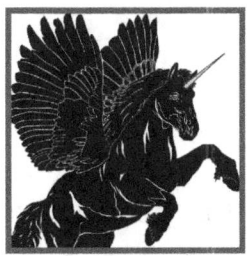

Alicorn Press

Soddy Daisy, TN. 37379

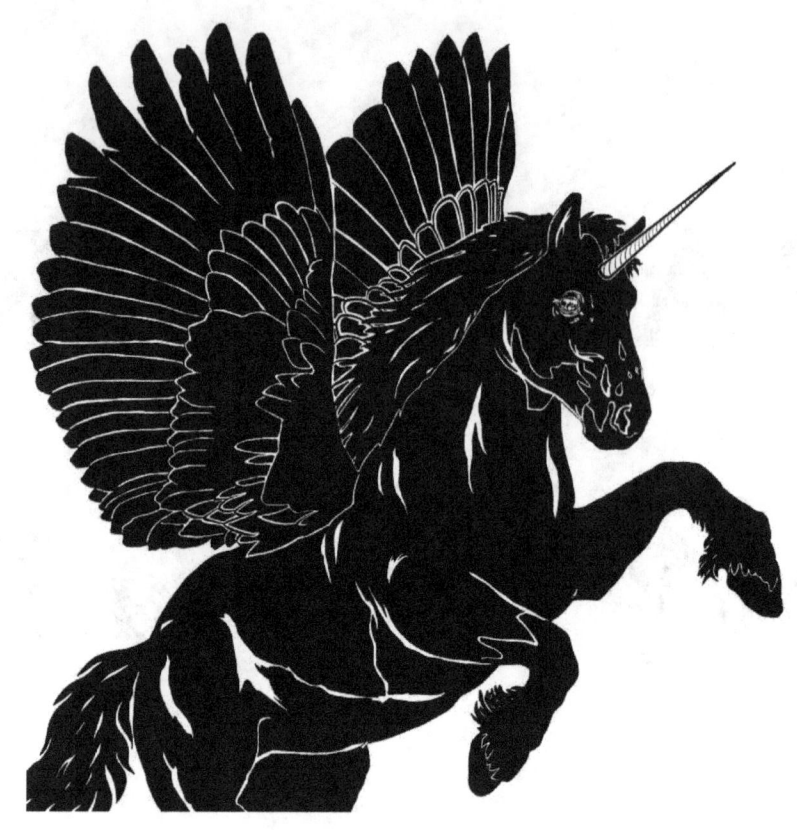

**Alicorn Press**

Soddy Daisy, TN. 37379

ISBN-13: 978-0692639856

# Coloring Tips:

Place a blank sheet of paper
under the page you are coloring.

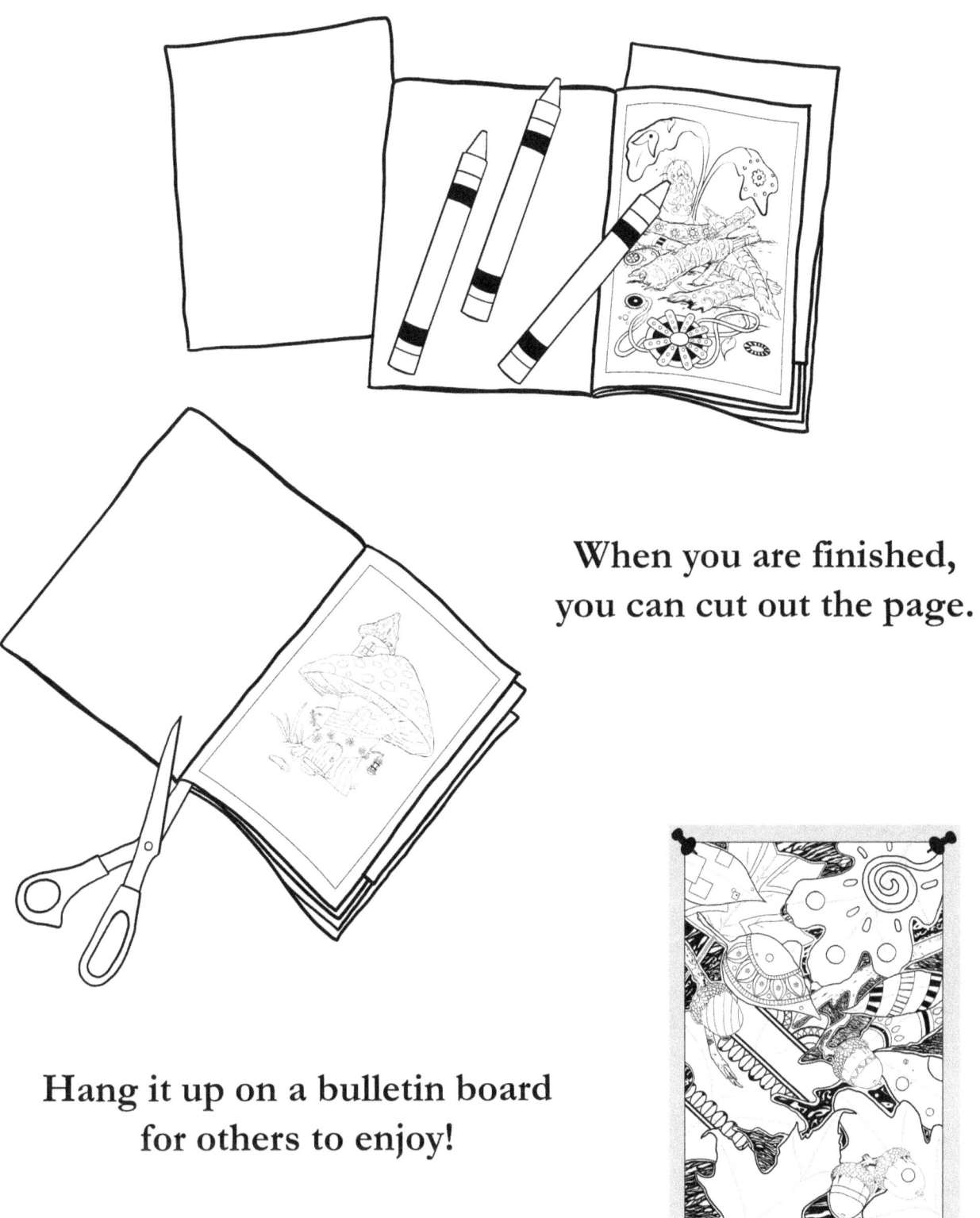

When you are finished,
you can cut out the page.

Hang it up on a bulletin board
for others to enjoy!

This book is for the light and love of my life, my wife Dawn.

Always Dawn.

# AUTHOR'S NOTE:

I would be remiss if I didn't take a moment to thank those of you who have purchased this book. While I have spent a lifetime drawing and painting, this is my first foray into the world of coloring books. I hope that you enjoy coloring these images as much as I did creating them. More than that, I hope that you'll share your creations with me either via my Facebook page or by sending me an e-mail. I would love to see the art and talent you bring to these pages.

I hope that filling these pages with color not only brings you joy, but that that the process also fills you with surprise and wonder.

Thank you for joining me on this journey.

Good luck!

John Ward
Soddy Daisy, Tennessee
February 7, 2016

# DEDICATION:

The theme for this book is an outgrowth of childhood nostalgia. As a young child, my grandmother and great aunt taught me all of the folklore and traditions that they had learned from their mother. These beliefs came from a spectrum of sources. Some were outright superstition. Others family tradition. Many times, the ideas could be traced back to hard won truths that some great forebear had learned, and passed down through the generations until it eventually traveled with them to America.

These ideals and philosophies primed my imagination and made me ready for the folklore that I would learn from one of my first baby sitters: my aunt Shirley. I can't say that she introduced me to mythology or to creatures like fairies, goblins and trolls. It was the mid '70's. Those creatures were already well on their way to leaving behind their homes in obscure books. They had transitioned to the silver screen and inspired many songs... entire albums of music. No, she wasn't the first person to talk to me about elves, but she was willing to sit and talk to me with the same degree of interest and enthusiasm that my young mind brought to those topics. Most of the time, our conversations began with me thumbing through the pages of her well-worn copy of *Time Life's Mysteries of the Unknown*. Those books were jumping off points for conversations that were just as labyrinthine as any maze that you would find on the ancient isle of Crete.

Naturally, I am forever indebted to my parents. My mother spent countless nights working with me as I struggled to learn how to read and spell. She gave me the foundation on which everything else has been built.

My father, though, was the one who showed me the value of the

fundamental skills that I had learned from my mother. My first lessons in appreciating story happened on Saturday afternoons, when we would watch syndicated versions of the old Flash Gordon serials together. Later, it was hearing stories about Odysseus, Hector, Troy, the Cyclops, Agamemnon, and a host of other characters who sparked my imagination. He read me my first horror story... right before I was put to bed. Despite that seeming lapse in judgment, the man did teach me to love stories and to love reading. It was his greatest gift to me.

If this book has any merit, it's a result of their investment in me. Any flaws, are due to my own personal failings.

Craddock had made a mistake. A horrible mistake that forever changed his life. He fell asleep in the wrong place. He didn't think that fairy circles had any power over leprechauns.

He was wrong.

Time works differently in those circles. While he slept, empires rose and fell. The world changed. His people moved on.

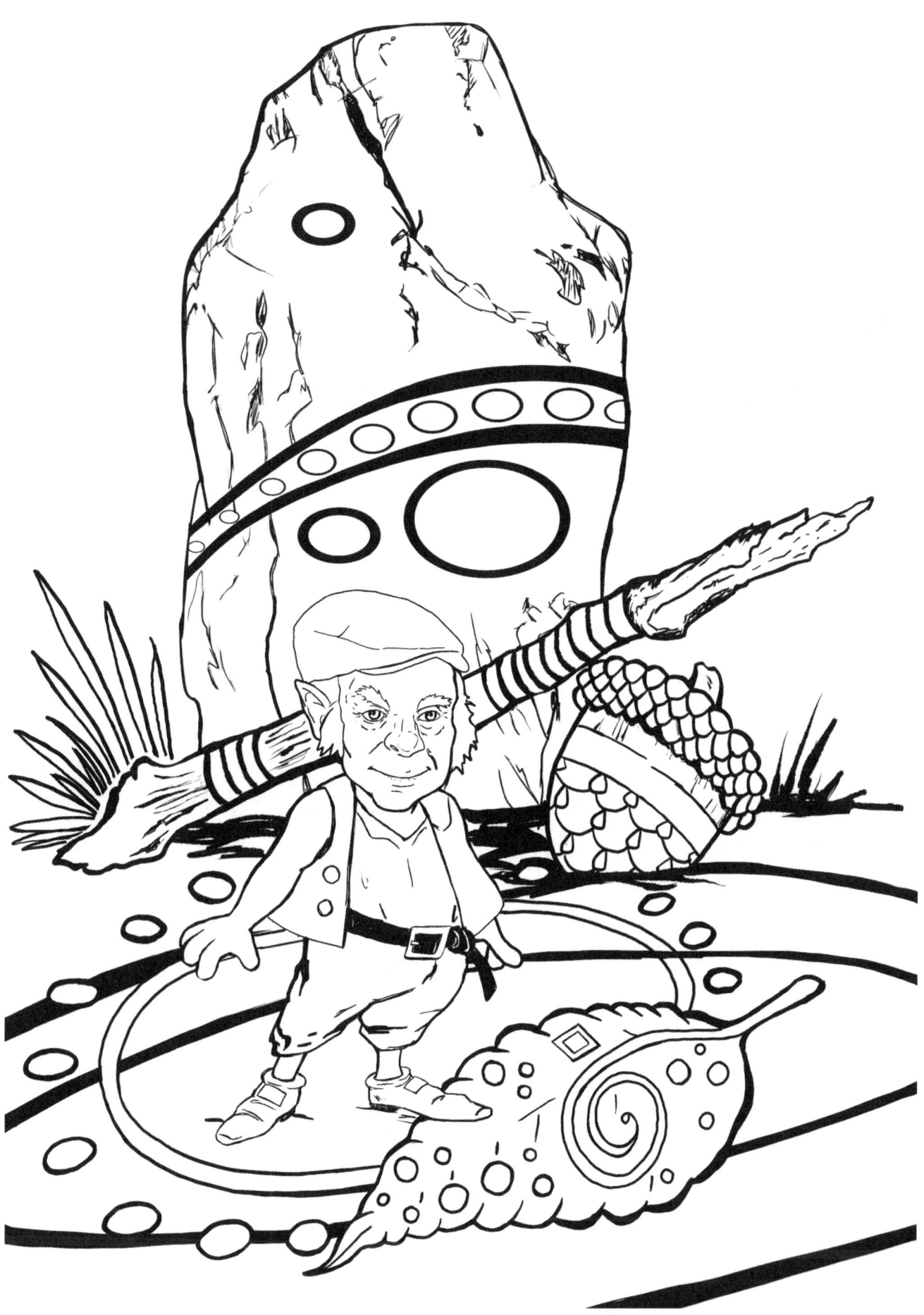

That midday nap lasted a thousand years. The hollow hills, where he had once made his home, had undergone gentrification.

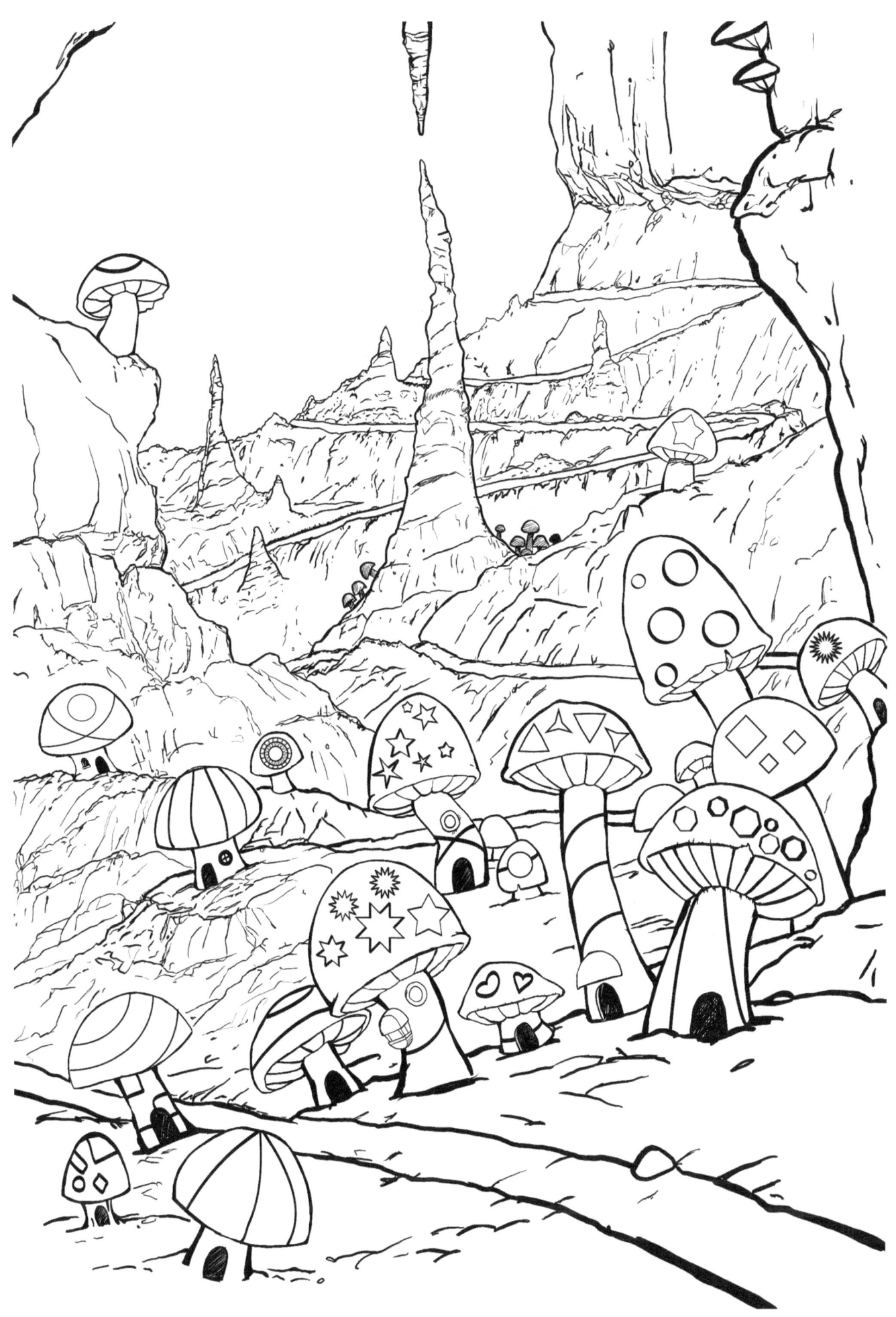

The cozy hollows and dens had been replaced by a growing subdivision of mushrooms. Pixies had taken up residence in the old neighborhood. All of the stately buildings had been torn down and replaced by brightly colored mushrooms.

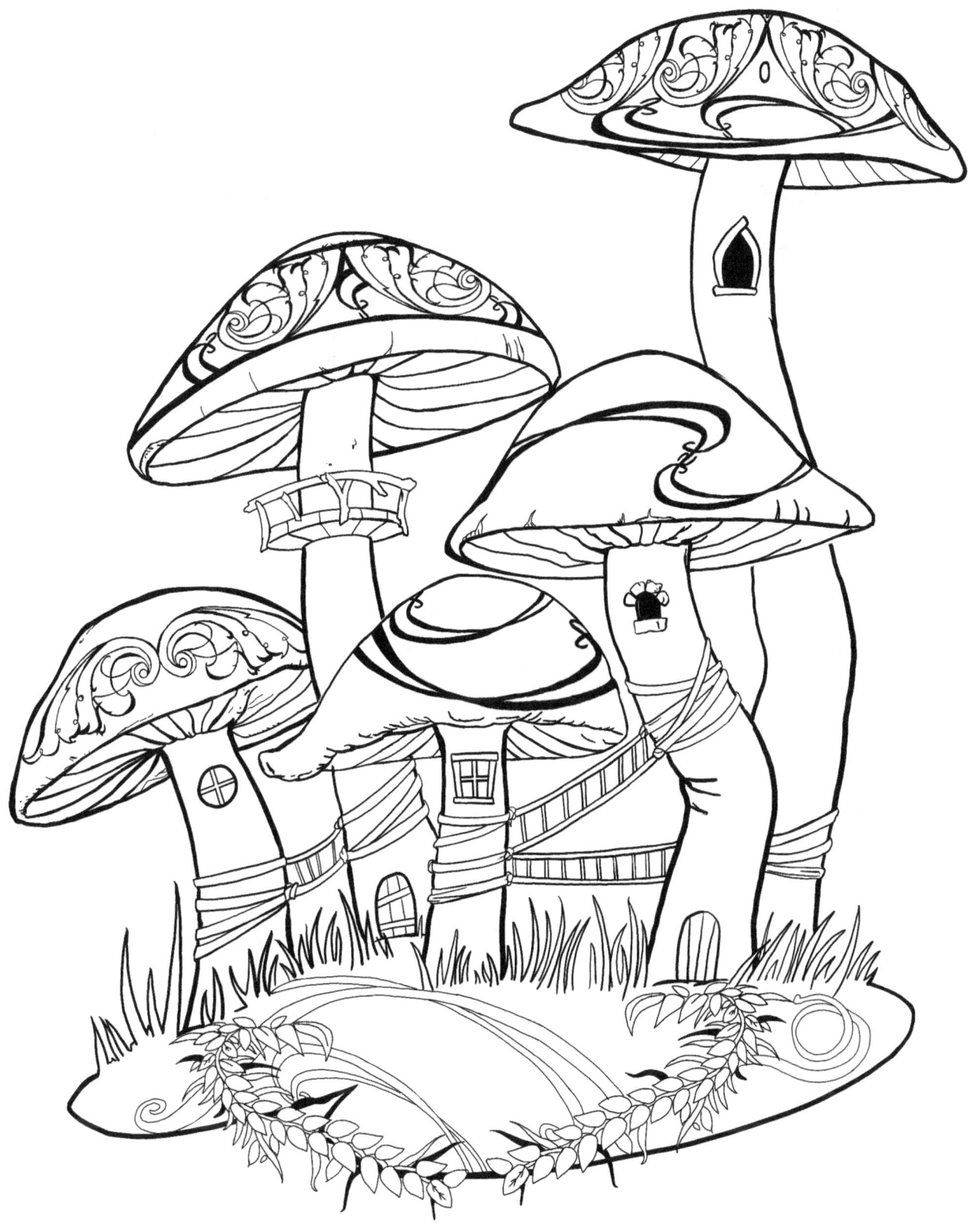

The old neighborhood was overrun by pixies, but Craddock still had hope. Maybe he'd have more luck finding some of his clan members outside if he went outside the city walls.

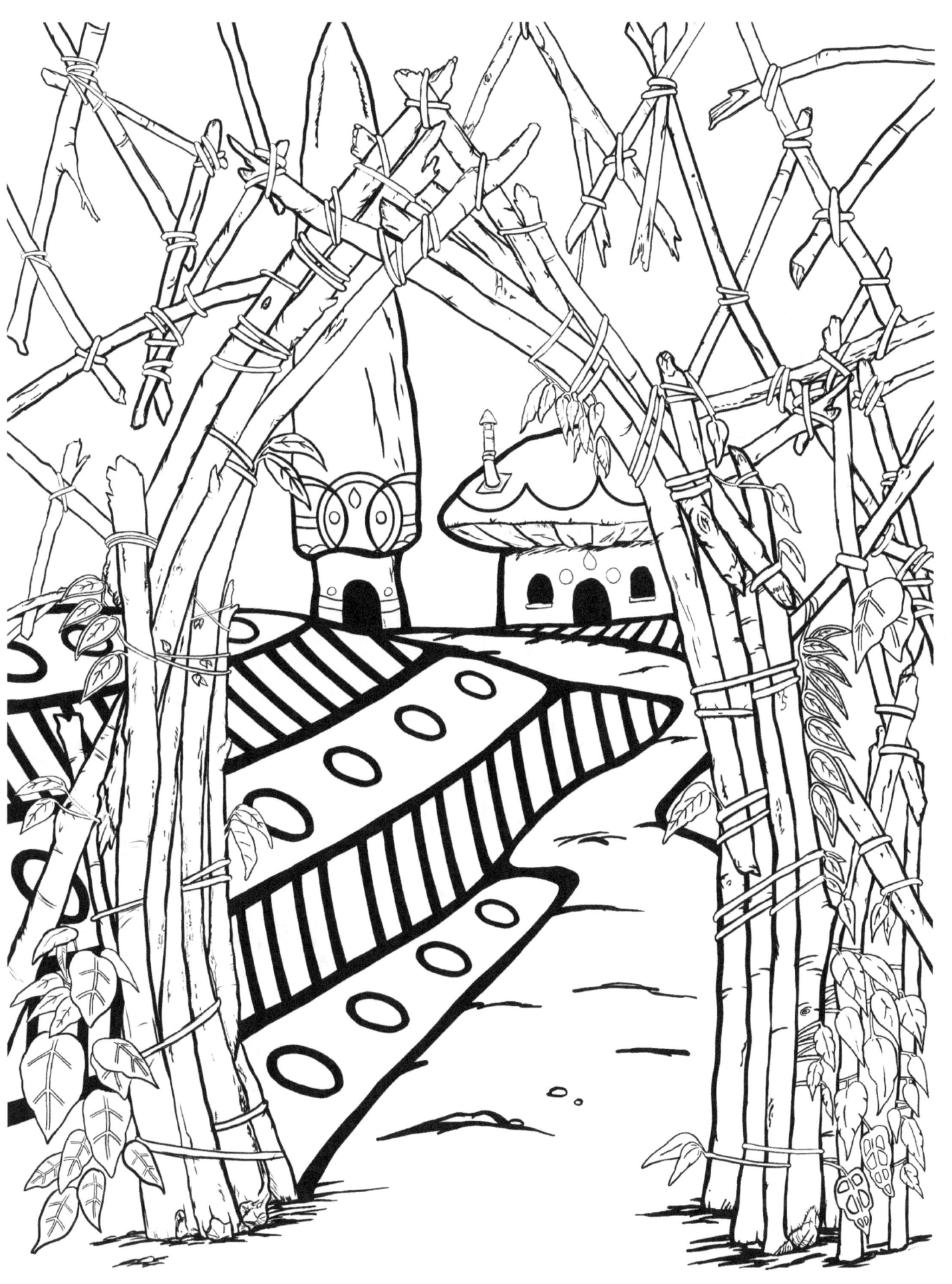

He went to the houses on the outskirts. First, he tried the home of Dabney. He knew that Dabney no longer lived there by the happy songs that filled the air. If this had been Dabney's home, his arrival would have been met with shouts and name calling. At least, until Dabney figured out that it was Craddock.

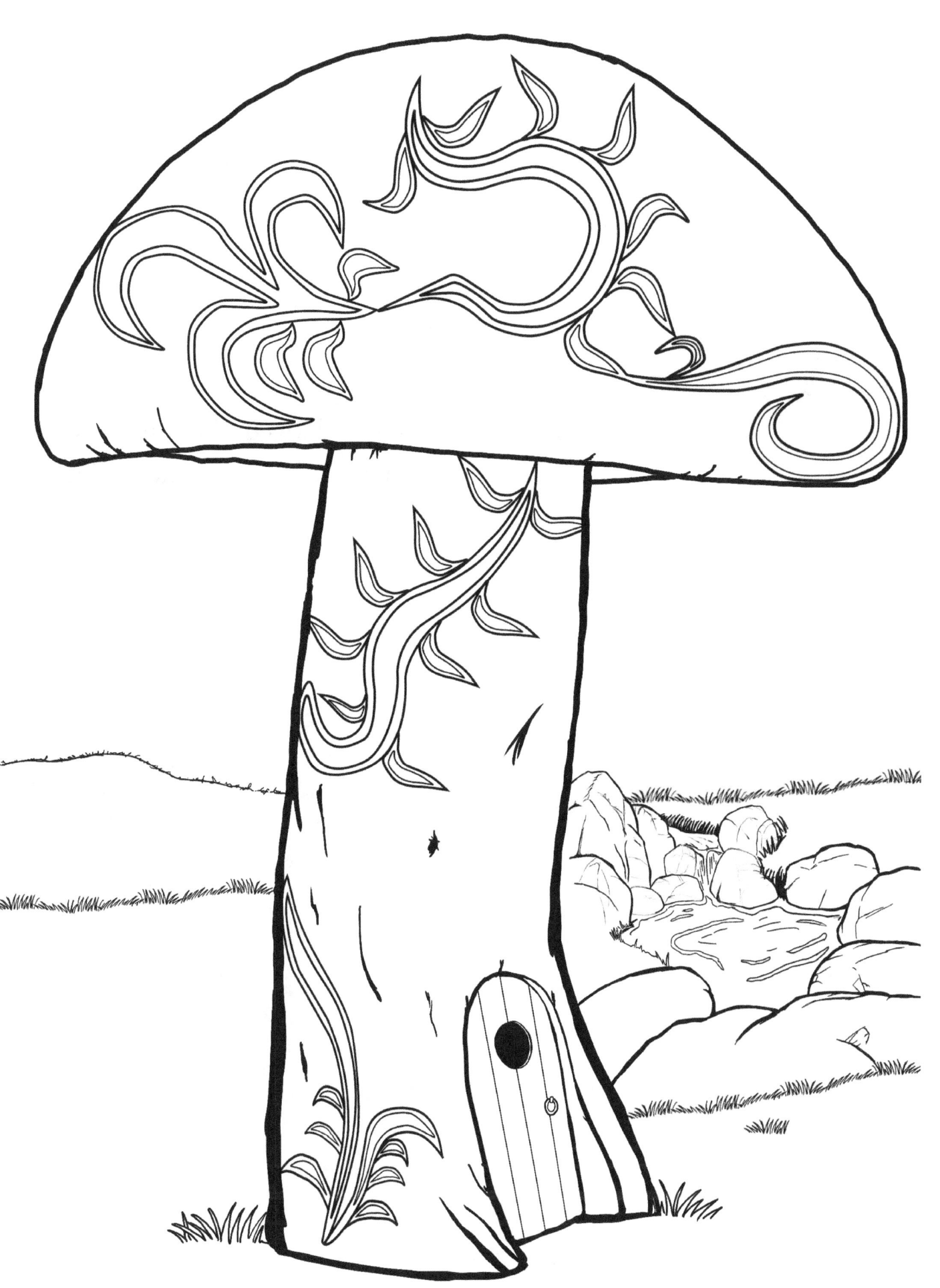

Next, he visited Fiona. In the spring of his youth, before Craddock had lost his hair, she had loved him. Maybe she still had enough kindness in her heart to tell him where all the leprechauns had gone, but she wasn't there.

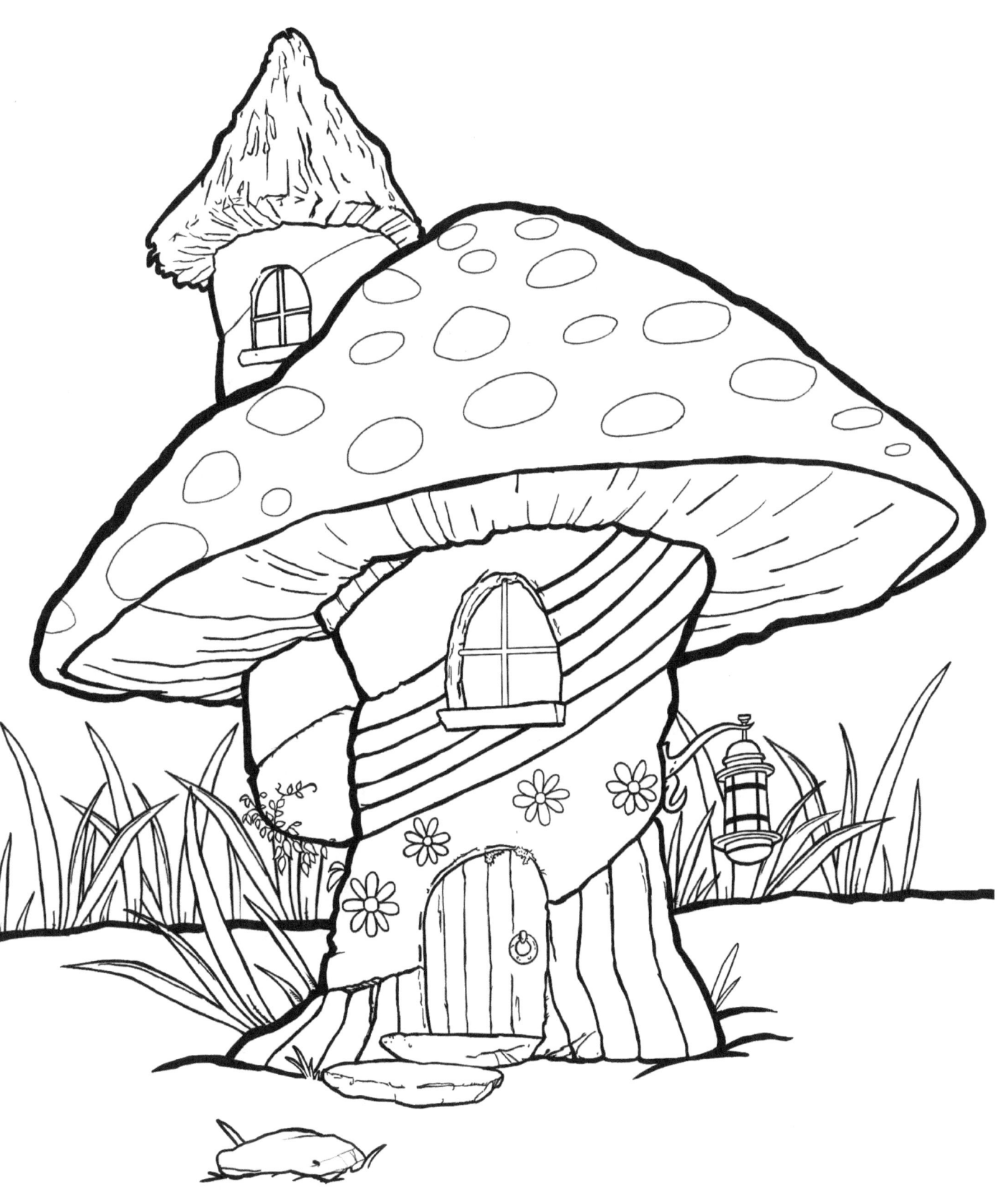

Craddock went to one last place. It wasn't really a home so much as a hideaway that he and his friends had found as children. He hoped that some of those old friends have gone there for shelter, but it too was abandoned.

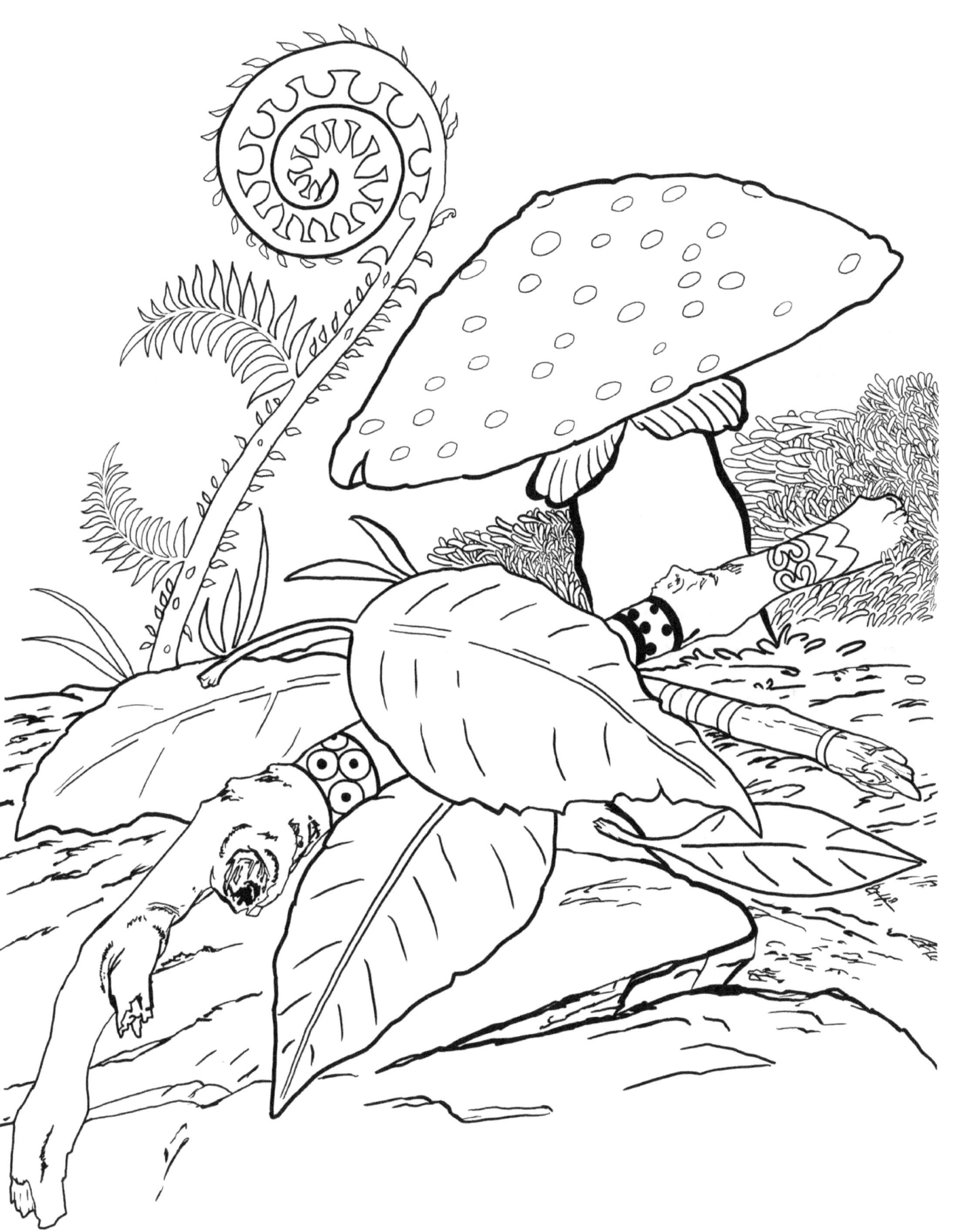

While he wandered through the forest, he chanced upon what appeared to be another fairy ring. "Perhaps," he thought, "I can go back to my own time." So, he crossed into the fairy ring and took a nap, but the only thing he got in return was a sore neck from sleeping on the leaves.

It wasn't a fairy ring at all. The patterns were designs that had been created by the pixies.. They were only designs that had been drawn on dead sticks and leaves and contained no magic.

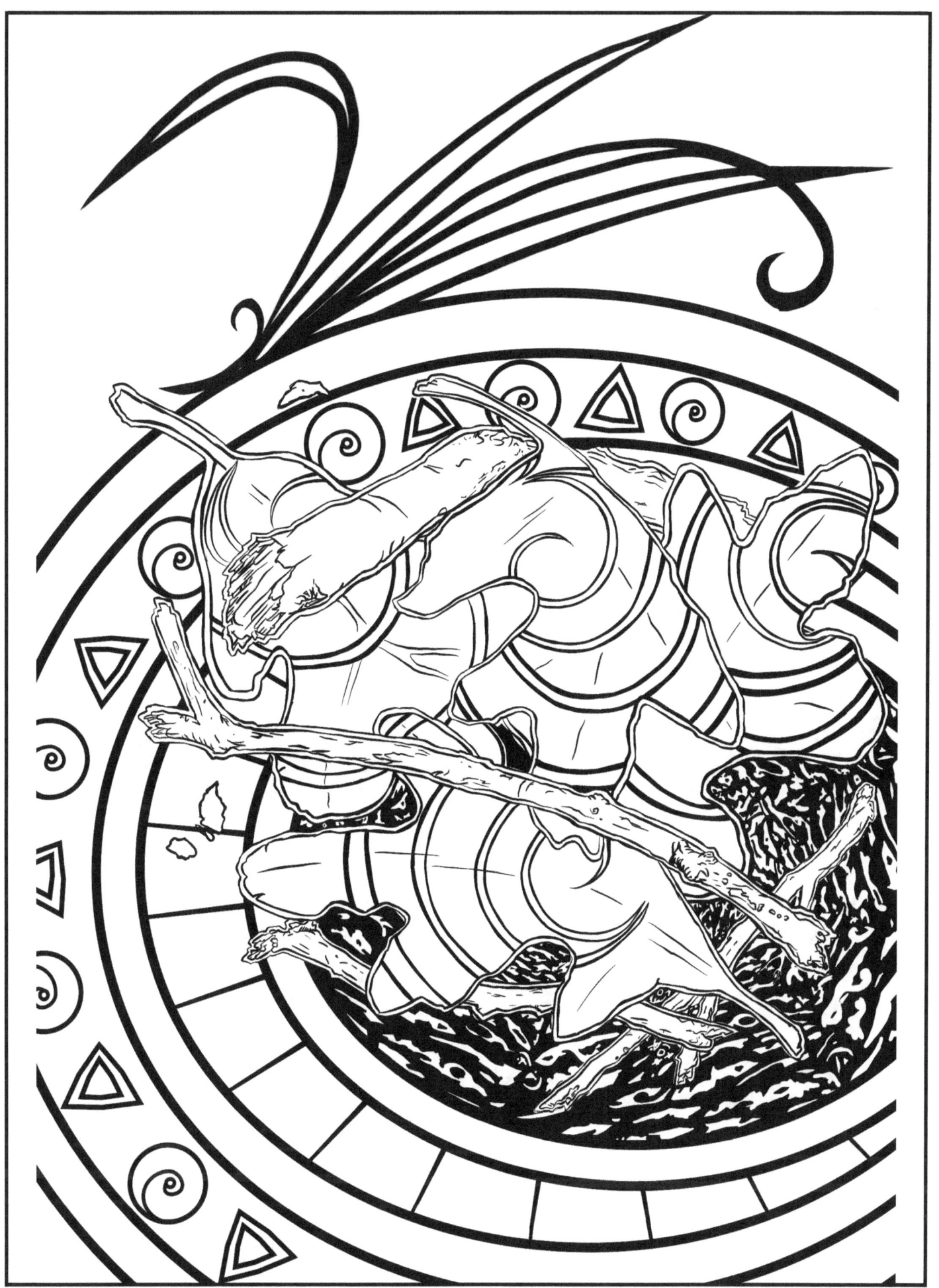

Craddock spied a ladybug sitting on a daisy. He thought to ask her whether she had seen the missing leprechauns, but she wasn't feeling talkative and didn't respond.

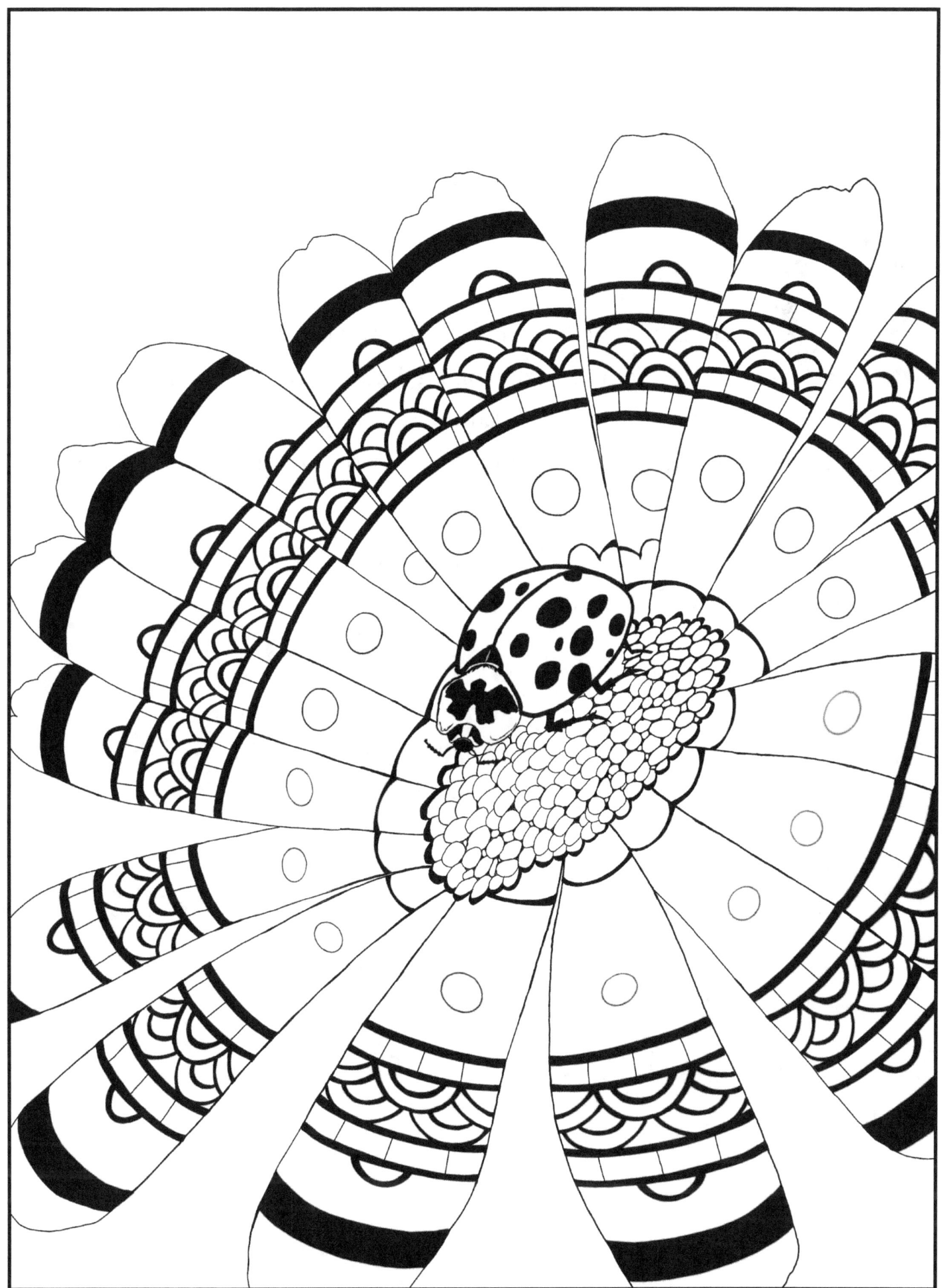

Discouraged, he left the ladybug behind. It wasn't long, however, until he met a caterpillar. The caterpillar had no knowledge of leprechauns or where they might be, but he thought he knew someone that might. "Go ask the dragon," the caterpillar said.

Craddock had only ever heard of one dragon in this area. Could it be the same one? He had to find out.

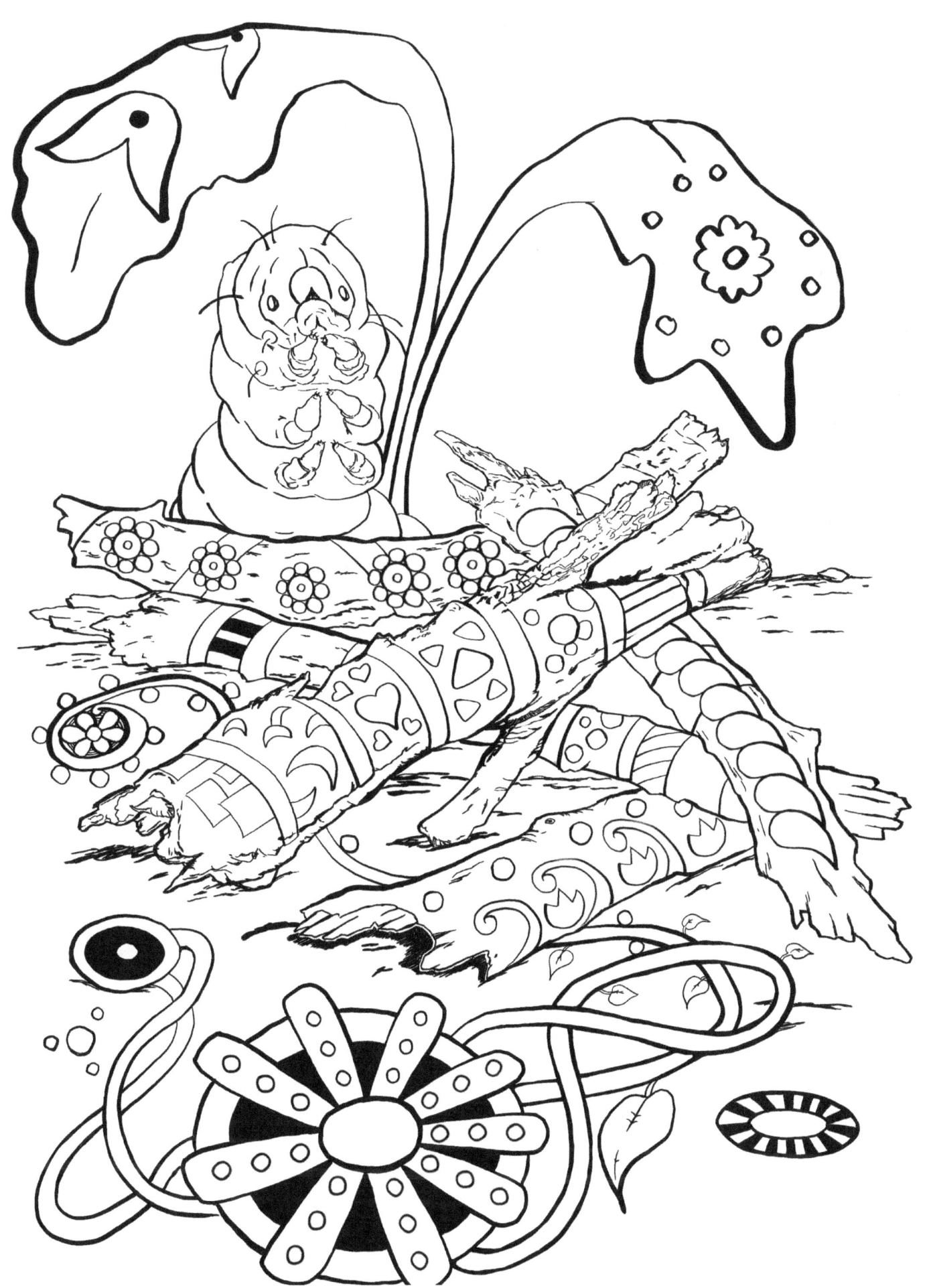

Craddock couldn't believe his eyes. It was the same dragon! More incredible, though, was the fact that the dragon was still a baby.

"Dragons live a very long time and age very slowly," the dragon told him with a slow smile. "Now, as to your friends. They've left. It seems that most of them bought timeshares in the Cayman Islands. Only pixies live here now."

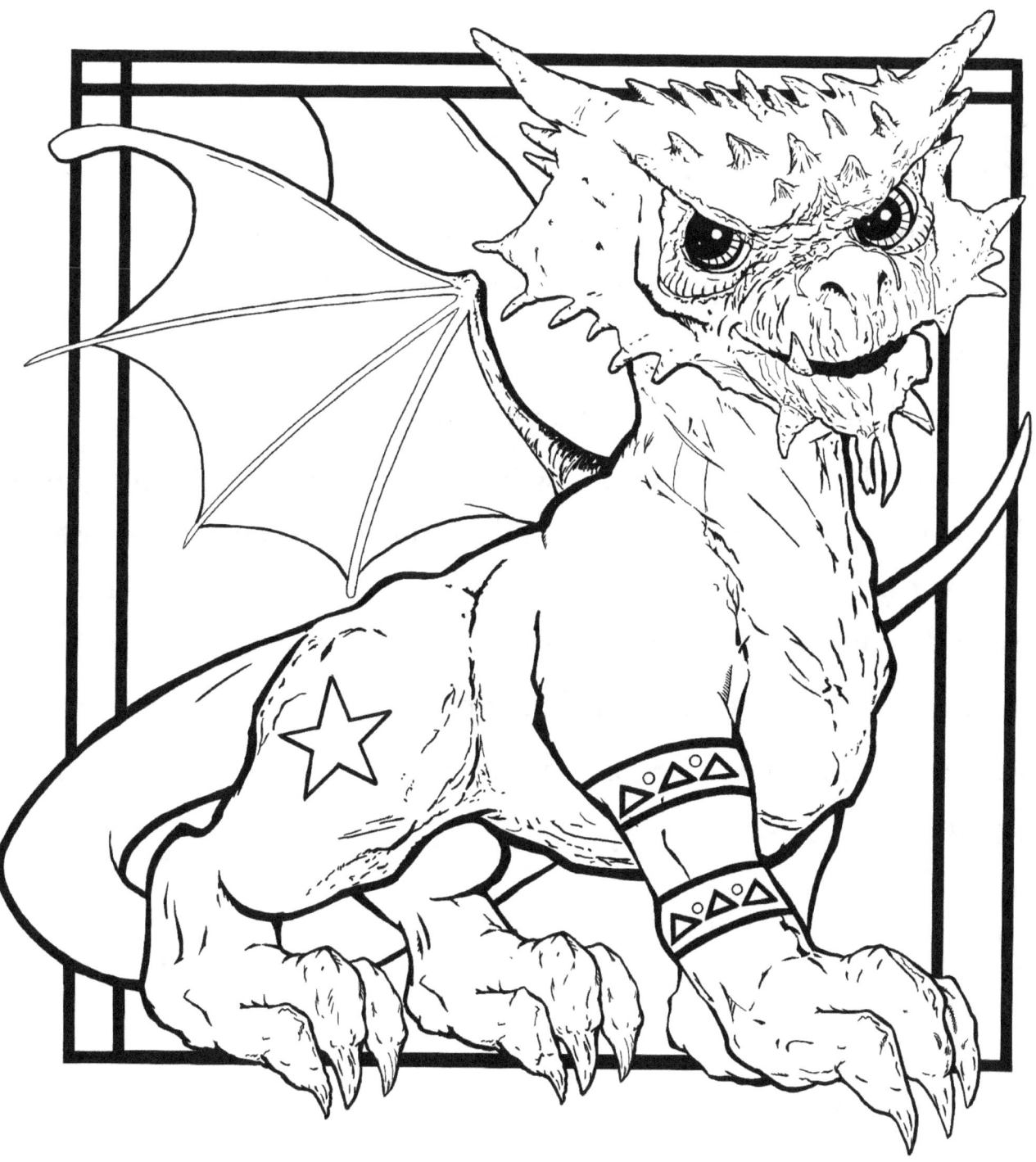

The news devastated Craddock. He walked through the forest for hours. He couldn't believe that they had left him behind. Eventually, he heard a low voice call out to him from above. He looked up and saw a snail perched precariously on a leaf.

"Why so glum, friend?"

Craddock explained how all of his people had left him behind.

The snail smiled at this. "Do you know how many times I've been left by my friends? Being left behind is what snails do." The snail seemed to pause to allow his words to sink in and to make sure Craddock understood. Finally, he said, "I've learned that it's okay to make new friends."

"But, but… they are all so happy. All the time."

"There are nice and interesting people everywhere you look. Even among happy pixies."

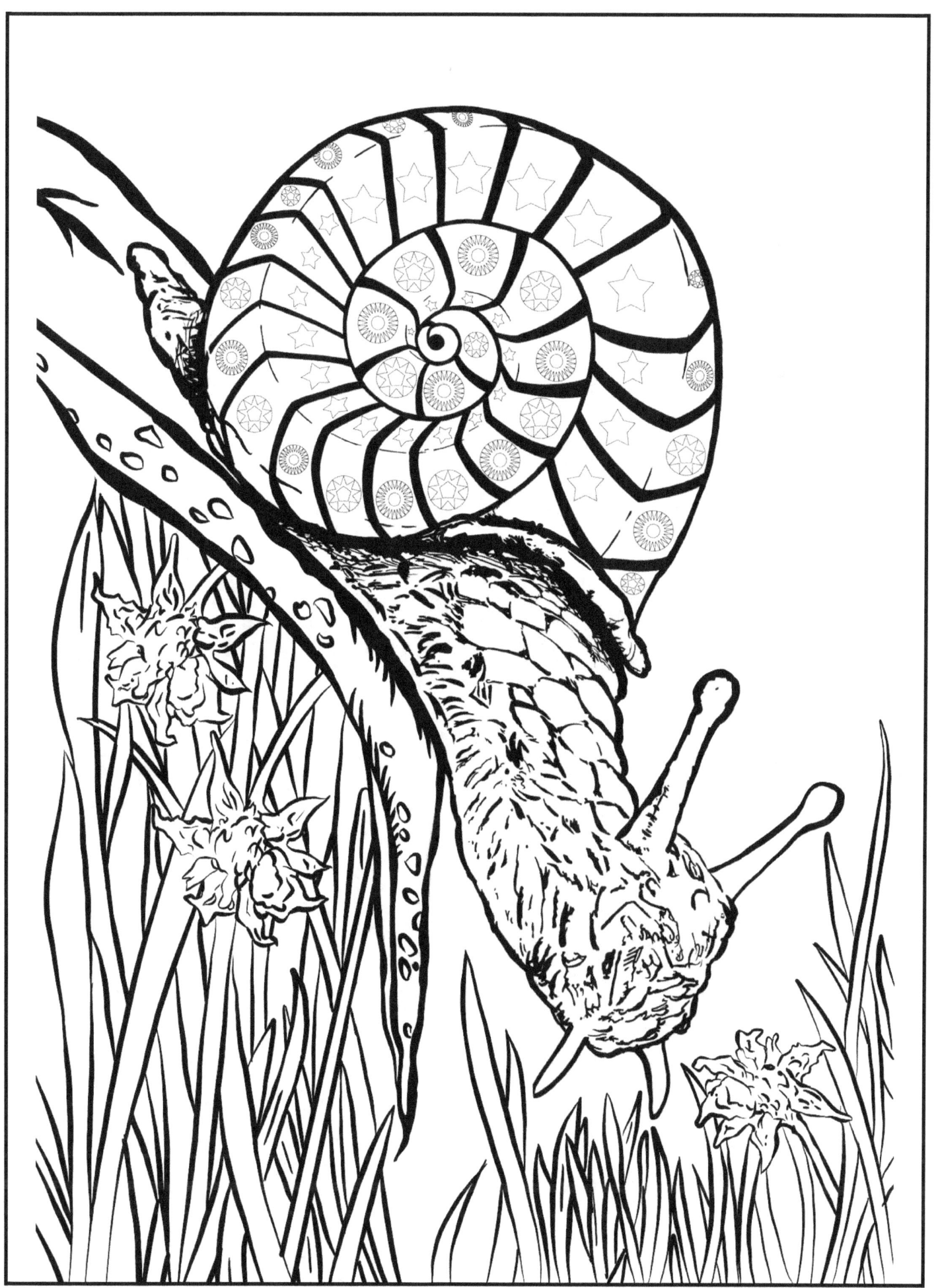

He noticed other designs. In fact, once he'd noticed them, they seemed to be everywhere.

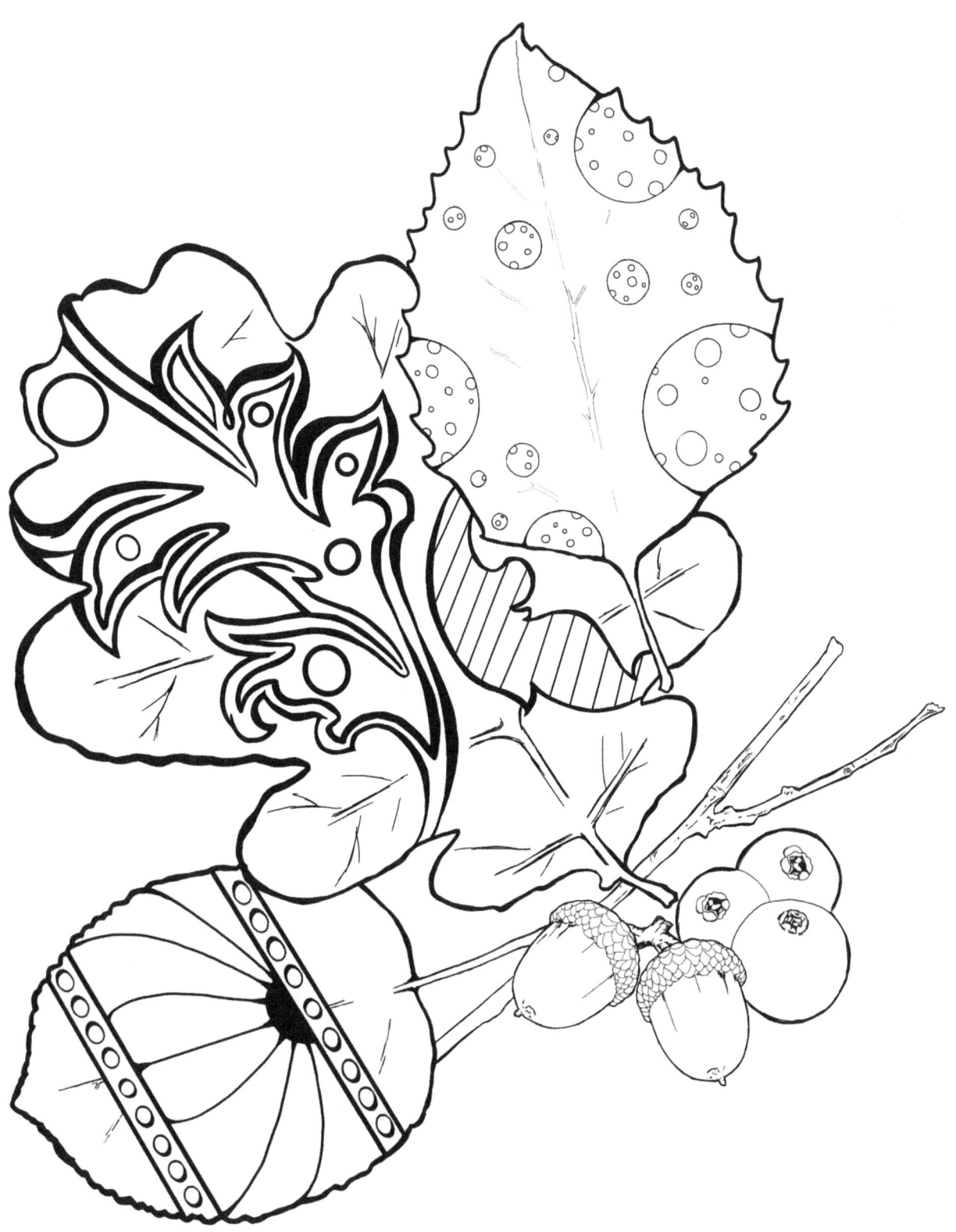

The closer he got to the mushroom city in which the pixies lived, the more intricate the patterns became.

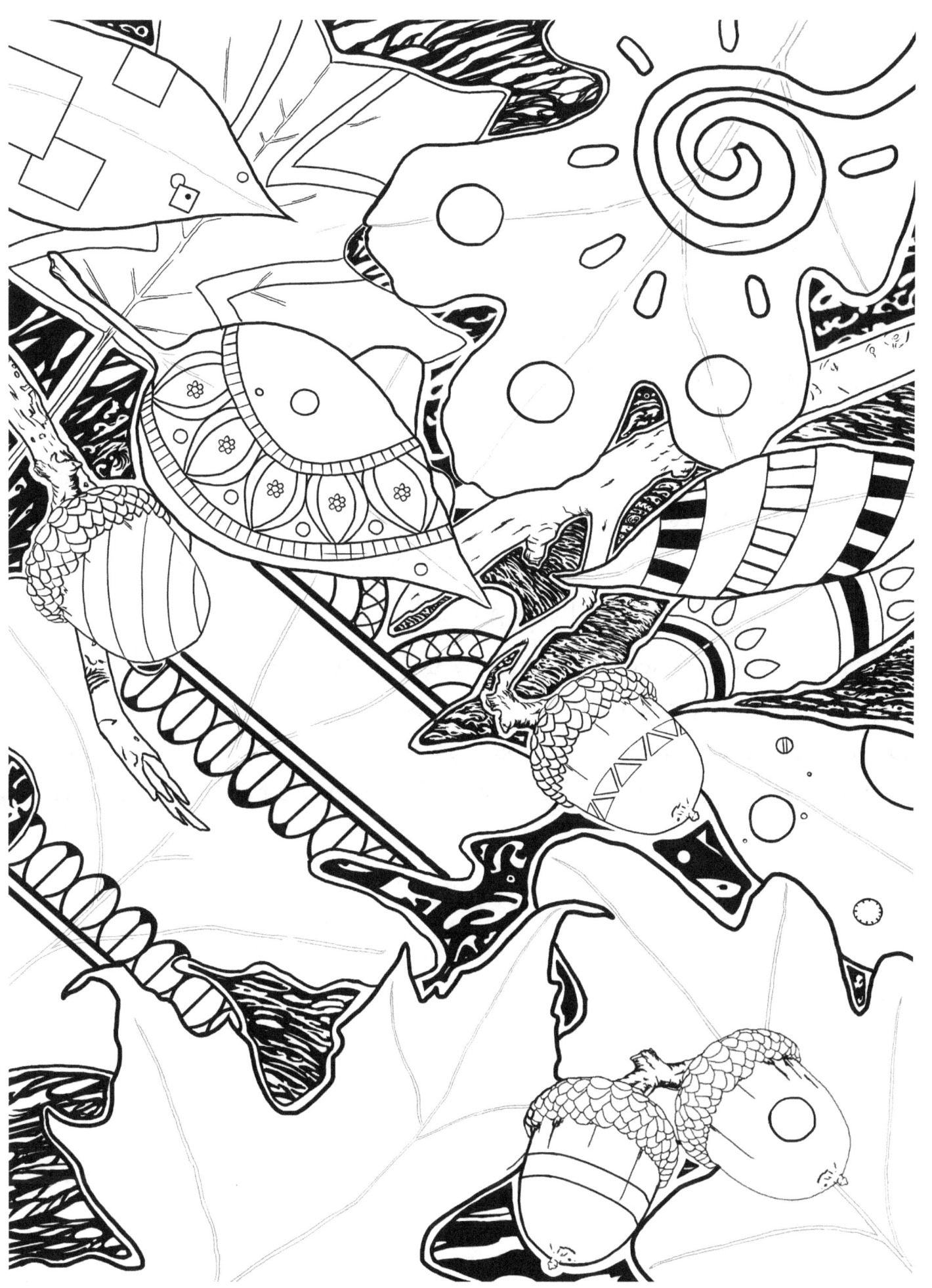

He was met outside the city by a delegation of pixies: Breena, Donella, and Kheelan. They explained that they had heard about his dilemma and how they wanted to help.

They brought him pots filled with paint and offered to allow him to come live among the pixies in their mushroom city. They were curious about what new patterns and designs he could add to the world around them.

"But, I'm not an artist," Craddock protested.

His objections didn't seem to matter to any of the pixies. Eventually, one of them stepped forward to explain, "There is no right or wrong when it comes to art. You listen to the voice in your heart and create what you will. Each person creates art that is unique to them. You can add beauty to the world, Craddock."

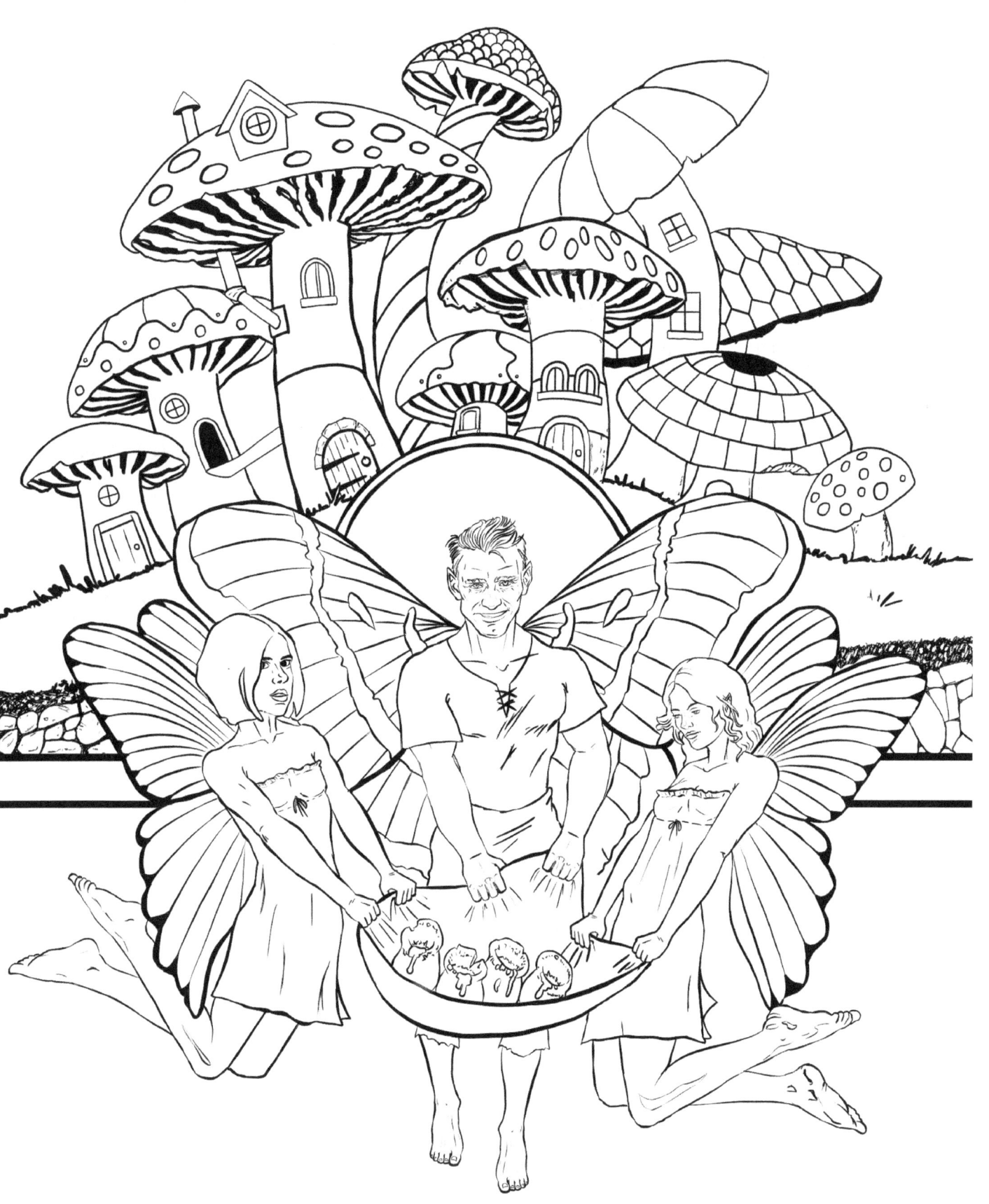

And, so, he considered their offer. Living among the pixies would be very different than the life he had known when he was surrounded by his clan. Would he be able to adapt? They had already seemed to accept him. Could he find happiness and peace here? Could he find a way to put up with their interminable singing? And then, he asked himself the most important question of all: "What other choice did he have?"

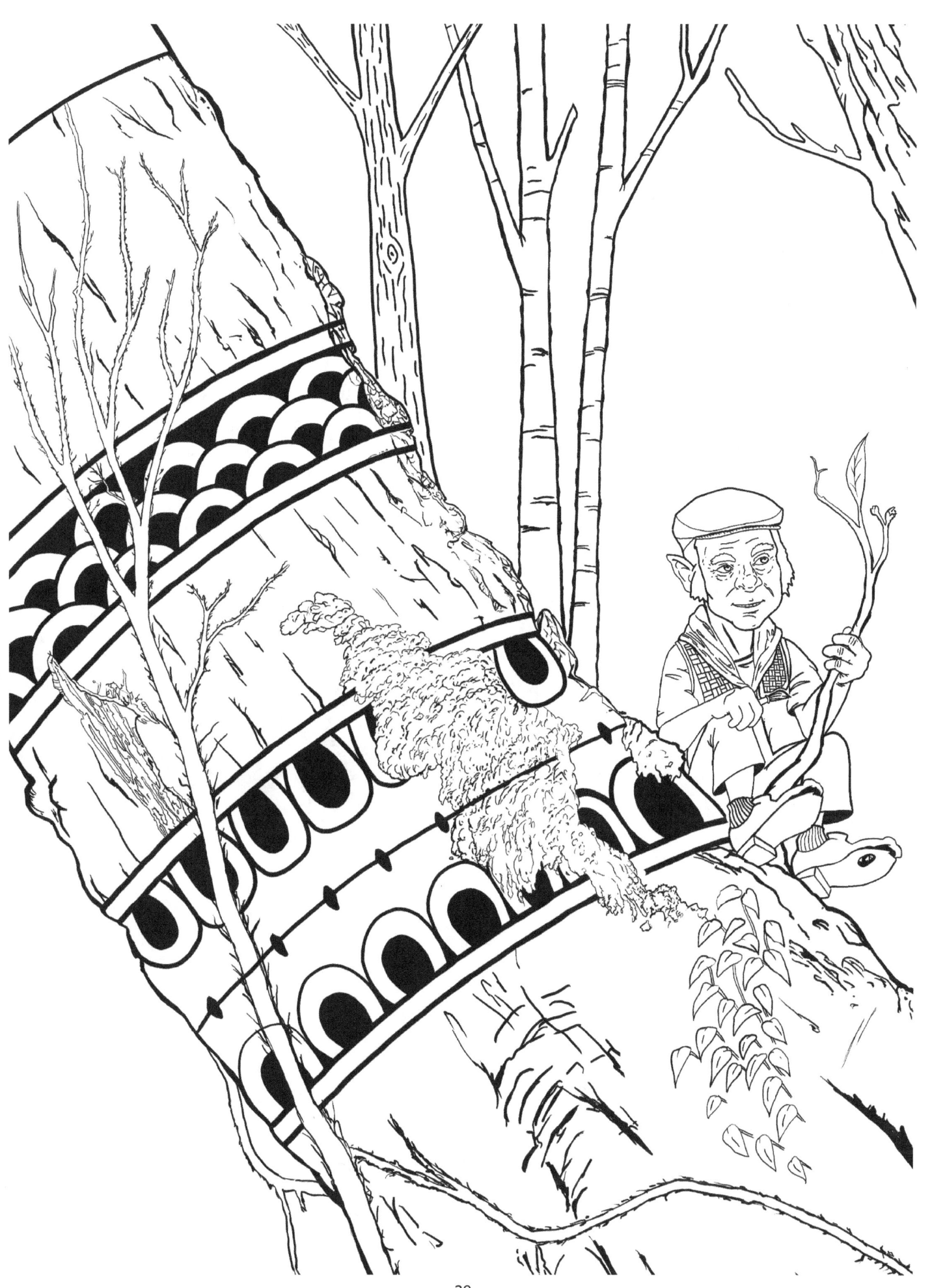

He decided to try.

At first, he focused on plants. The work was easy. The designs were simple. He found leaves to be a particularly inviting canvas.

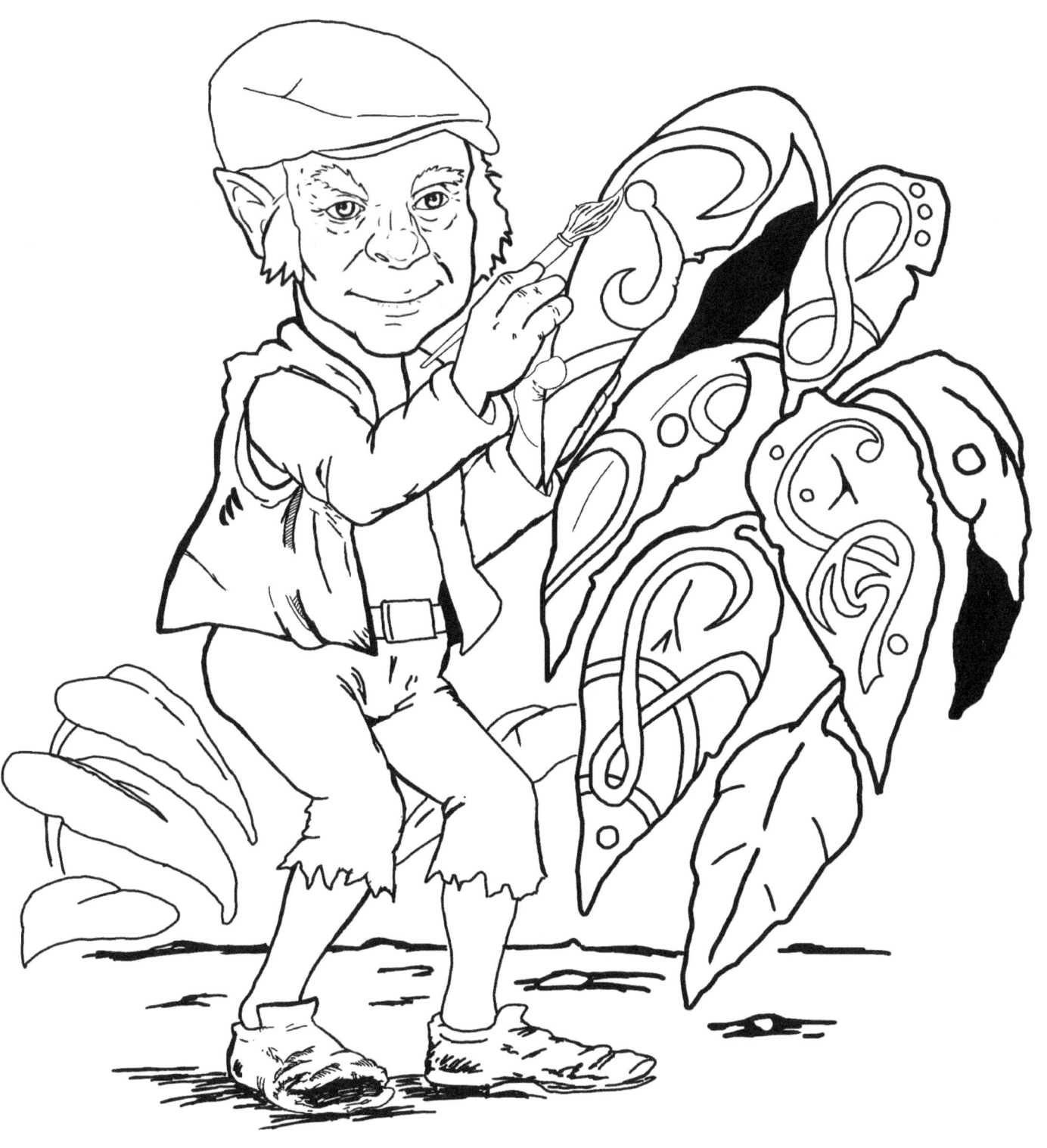

As more and more people expressed appreciation for his work, his confidence grew. With greater confidence, came increased happiness and a willingness to be more expressive.

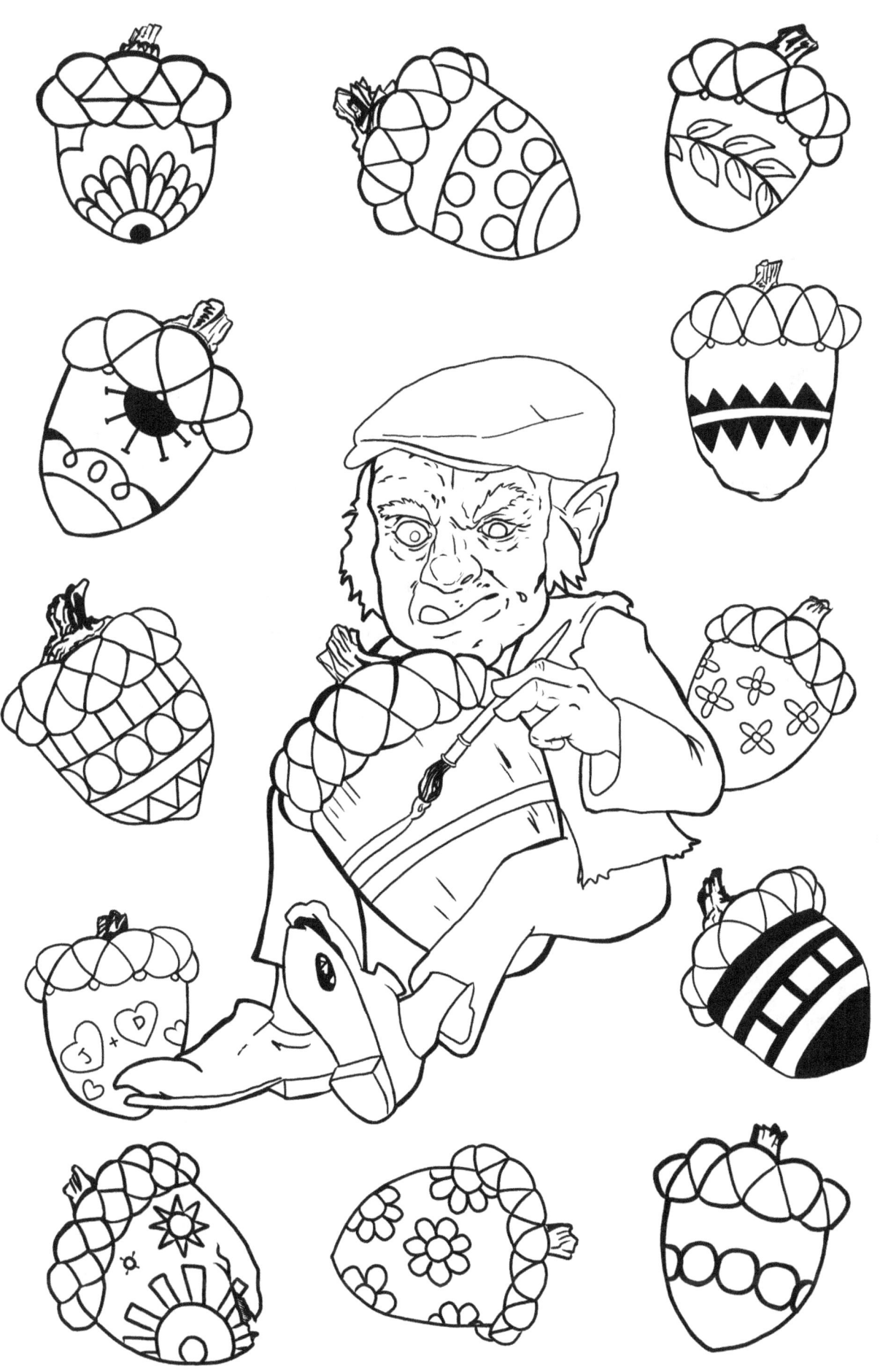

He moved on to larger and larger projects. It wasn't long until he discovered the type of work that brought him the most happiness. He discovered that adding drawings and designs to mushroom houses gave him a sense of pride. There was something about defining the look of an entire neighborhood that made him feel accomplished.

The work also carried with it an unexpected benefit. The pixies would leave him to work on their homes in solitude. The quiet helped him to focus and more than that, it gave him respite from their endless songs.

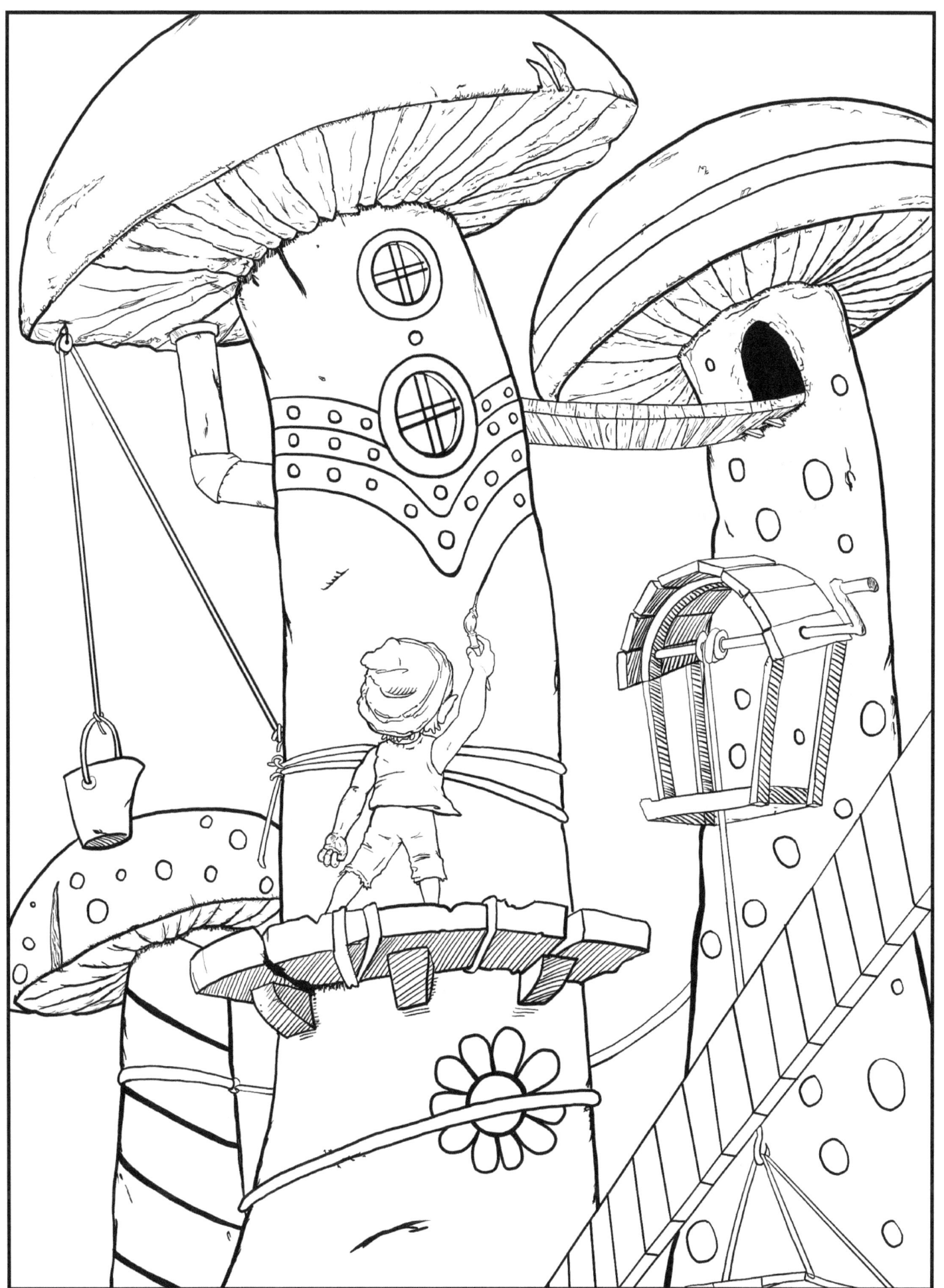

As an expression of their gratitude for all of his work, the pixies planted a shamrock pattern in Craddock's lawn. Life without his clan wasn't the same, but some days— every now and then— it could be better. Now, if he could just get the pixies to stop trying to teach him to sing.

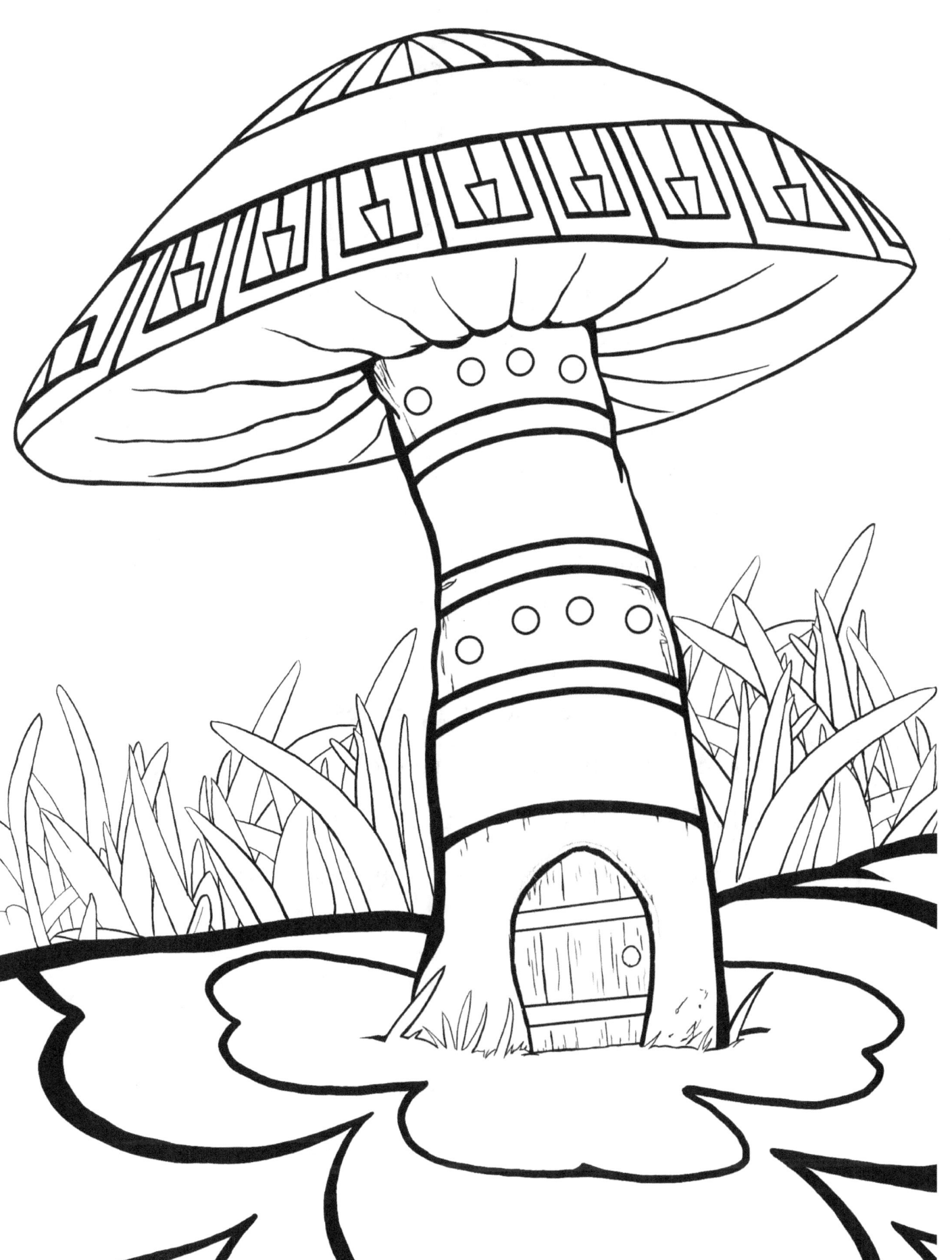

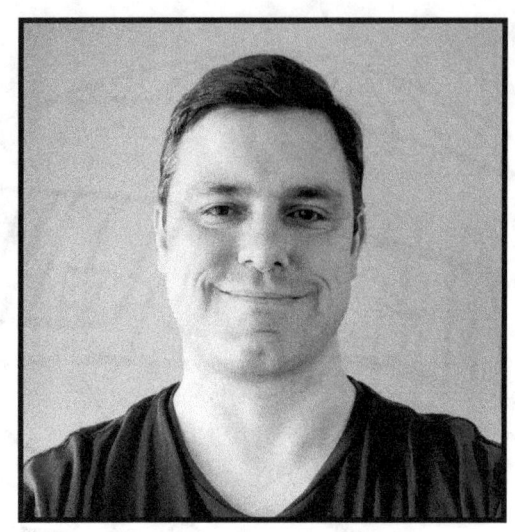

## About the Author

John Ward is an illustrator in Soddy Daisy, Tennessee. He divides his days doing illustration work for clients, chasing his young daughters around the house, and trying to keep his dachshund as happy as his wife. He has a history of spending an inordinate amount of time on social media, but he's in a program for that.

~

## Free Coloring Pages

John would love to hear from you at john@alicornpress.com

Send your feedback and suggestions, or post a review on Amazon.

You will receive free coloring pages that are guaranteed to brighten your day.

## Website:

www.alicornpress.com

## Facebook page:

https://www.facebook.com/alicornpress/

## Acknowledgements

Thank you to Kate Harper for her endless nagging and haranguing.

Without her, this book would have been published much later.

Seriously though, Kate, you can stop harassing me now.

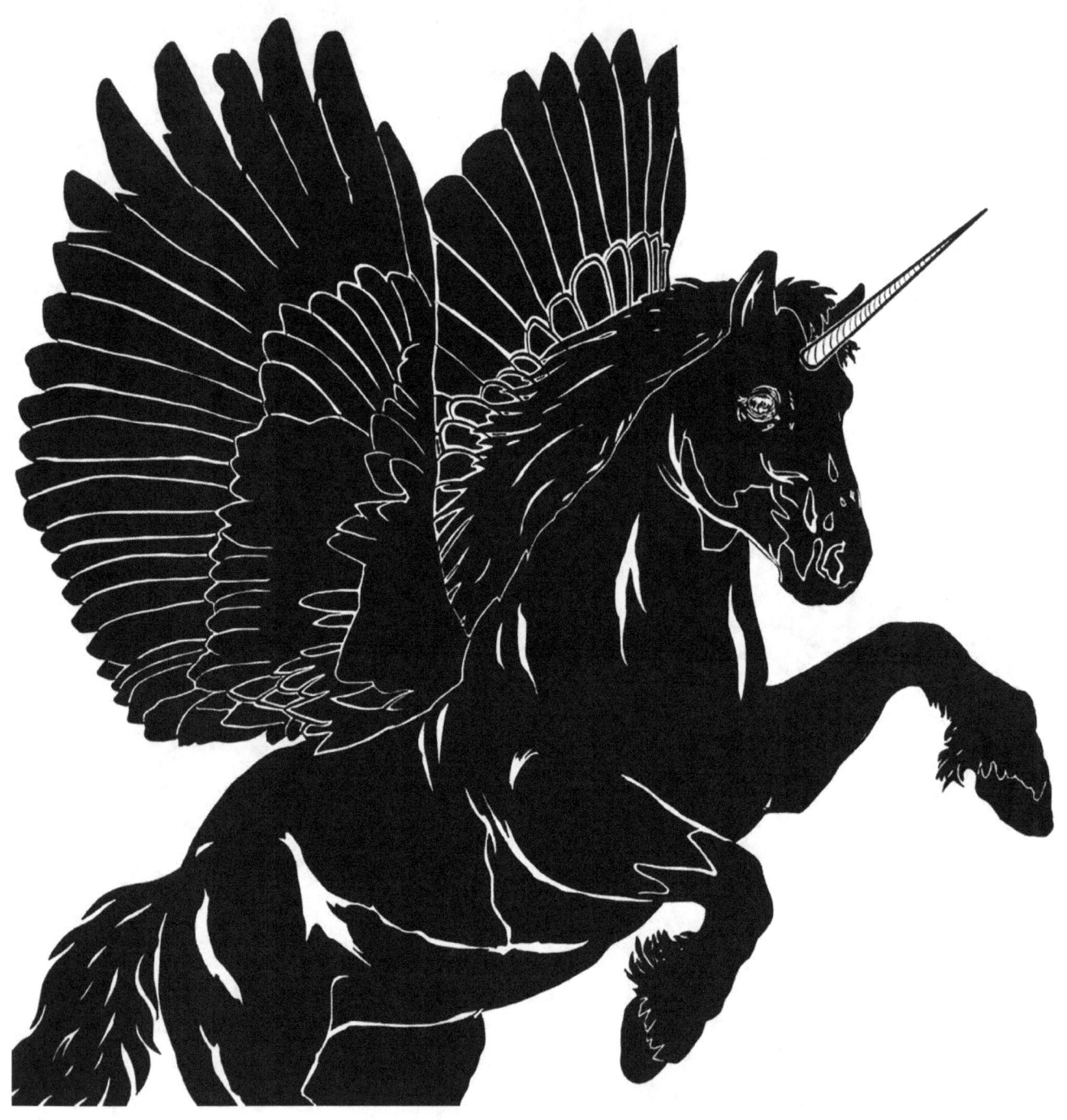

**Alicorn Press**

www.alicornpress.com

www.ingramcontent.com/pod-product-compliance
Lightning Source LLC
Chambersburg PA
CBHW080846170526
45158CB00009B/2646